if anybody asks me...

1,001 Questions
for educators, counselors and therapists

Larry Eckert

Published by:

Wood 'N' Barnes Publishing
2309 N. Willow, Ste. A
Bethany, OK 73008
(800) 678-0621

1st Edition © 1998, Wood 'N' Barnes Publishing.
All rights reserved.

2009 Edition, Wood 'N' Barnes Publishing.
Questions were revised and updated in 2009.

Cover art by Blue Designs
Interior layout by Ramona Cunningham

Printed in the United States of America
Oklahoma
ISBN # 978-1-885473-24-0

For Heather,
whose insightful and inspiring poetry
will someday open the doors she is now
able to only look through. Her continual
dedication to the writing of verse will be a
pathway to answering many of
life's questions.

— About the Author —

Larry Eckert has a BA in Elementary Education from the University of Northern Iowa and an MA in School Counseling from the University of Iowa. He has 17 years experience as an elementary school teacher and guidance counselor working with minority and at-risk students as well as the general population. Larry has worked with students with physical and mental disabilities, both in institutional settings and public schools.

Contents

—— if anybody asks me...

Introduction

Adolescents have opinions! Believe it! They may not even be aware of their opinions, but they exist. Sometimes they are just below the surface, waiting to "erupt," other times they are unconscious and not fully thought out, conflicting with other ideas.

The 1,001 questions in this book are developed for young people ages 11 to 18. The questions can be used in either a small group, large group or same gender setting. They can be activity starters, discussion icebreakers, or "grist" for an entire session. In a group, introductory questions are an appropriate method to help members begin to focus and concentrate as a whole, as well as to experience differing opinions, and also to practice problem-solving methods.

Counselors, educators, group leaders, and parents can use questions from this list to help young people form personal opinions and have discussions with others, leading to greater understanding of themselves and their peers. Leaders will also gain greater insight into the unique teenage world. Listen to their reasoning! Their analysis is as valuable and important to understand as their answers.

Feel free to adapt, expand, or rephrase the questions to best suit your own situation.

Have fun and enjoy the experience!

—— if anybody asks me...

You

1. What would have to happen for you to feel that you are the luckiest person alive? Why?

2. What is your most prized possession? Why?

3. Who would you like to have visit you for a whole 24 hours? Why?

4. Would you rather be rich, famous, or happy? Why?

5. What one part of you—inner or outer—would you like to change? Why?

6. If your house was on fire, what one thing would you try to save? Why?

7. Which of your senses are the most important to you? Why?

8. Are you a person who likes constant change, or do you need things more stable and consistent? Why?

9. Your friends say, "Go for it!" What would you do?

10. What is a change you've made in yourself in the last year?

11. Would you like to be viewed by others as a hero? Why, or why not?

12. What is a good habit of yours?

13. What is a bad habit of yours?

14. What three words would you want others to use in describing you?

15. What instrument would you like to play well? Why?

16. What makes you laugh the most when you consider it?

17. What medication would you never want to take again? Why?

18. What is the most unusual sandwich you have ever made?

19. What are two ways you think you will change in the next five years?

20. Are there some secrets that should not be told to you? If so, which kind?

21. If you could have the world's largest collection of something, what would it be? Why?

22.   What was your last nightmare about?

23.   What would you say is a natural talent of yours–not learned or developed?

24.   What is one way you could be taking better care of yourself? What makes it hard to do?

25.   What is a habit you would like to change? Why?

26. What mood are you in the most often? Why?

27.   If you were someone else, and saw YOU walking down the street, what would you think? Why?

28.   What is something you have an addiction to? How can you tell?

29. Which organs (eyes, heart, kidney, etc.) would you be willing to donate to someone if you no longer needed them? Why?

30. If you could not watch any TV, how would you spend that time? Why?

31.   When you are home alone, what activity consumes most of your time? Why?

32. Do you usually play sports and other games just for the fun of it, or to really win? Why?

33. In which setting are you most natural—at school, with friends, or at home? Why?

34. Who is the person who has the most faith and confidence in your abilities? How does that person show it?

35. If you were going to be in a parade, how would you want to display yourself? Why?

36. If you could make yourself invisible, what would you most want to do? Why?

37. What premonition or dream about the future, have you had actually come true?

38. If you were to teach lessons to someone, what would the lessons be about? Why?

39. Do you like to make difficult decisions by yourself, or have someone else make them for (with) you? Why?

40. What is your favorite place to be when you must think about making a personal decision? What makes it so special?

41. Would you rather see a movie in a theater that is full of people or almost empty? Why?

42. If everyone had mental telepathy, and others could read your mind, would your own thoughts change? If so, in what way?

43. What makes your bedroom different from anyone else's that you know?

44. What is the most heroic deed you have done in your life? Would you do it again?

45. Who do you think would like to get to know you better right now?

46. What is the one accomplishment in your life about which you are the most proud? Why?

47. Are you more likely to take care of yourself, or take care of others first? Why?

48. When it comes to making decisions, do you usually need time to think things through, or do you mostly make decisions right away?

49. Considering the average condition of your bedroom, would you most likely be proud or embarrassed to have someone just drop by? Why?

50. Right now—today—who would you like to impress the most? In what way?

51. When you have to be given bad news, do you want to be told gently and a little at a time, or be told the whole story all at once? Why?

52. When and where are you the most at peace with yourself?

53. In what situations do you lack confidence in yourself? Why?

54. What is something that has happened in your life that you can explain only as a miracle? Why?

55. When you daydream, who or what do your thoughts turn to?

56. Are you more likely to give, or get, compliments? Why?

57. Are you more of a "night person" or a "day person"? Why?

58. Are you more pleased or uncomfortable with the secrets you are keeping to yourself right now? Why?

59. Could you do with more or less sleep than you are getting now? How can you tell?

60. What do you do to get over feeling "down" and sorry for yourself?

61. When you get voice mail or an answering machine, are you more likely to leave a message or simply hang up? Why?

62. What would you do with $5 at the convenience store?

63. For your next book report, are you more likely to read a larger book and write a longer report for an "A," or read a shorter book and write a brief report for an easy "C"? Why?

64. You are a famous person, and your popularity increases as photographers shoot and publish your pictures continually. Would you enjoy being photographed for your fans, or could it get to be a real nuisance? Why?

65. Which word in the dictionary should have your picture next to it as a perfect example? Why?

66. What is the most impulsive thing you have ever done? Why? What was the outcome?

67. Have you ever won a game and NOT felt good about it? Why, or why not?

68. The local station is going to videotape 30 consecutive minutes of your week to spotlight on TV. Which half hour would you want them to tape? Why?

69. What sound, when you hear it, just drives you up the wall? Why?

70. After five consecutive days of school, what do you most look forward to on the weekend? Why?

71. When you want to "mellow out," what song do you listen to? Why?

72. What is something you are saving your money for right now?

73. Do you voluntarily wear your seat belt without being reminded? Why, or why not?

74. What season of the year do you look forward to the most? Why?

75. If a movie of your life (so far) were going to be made, what would be the most appropriate title for it? Why?

76. If a movie of your life were to be made, who would be the best person to play "you"? Why?

77. If your family were to host a foreign exchange student for a year, what country would you like that student to be from? Why?

78. If you were going to be a foreign exchange student for a year, in which country would you most like to live? Why?

79. Your entire class has been chosen to go on a national talent show with each person giving an individual performance of his or her greatest talent. What would you choose as yours? Why?

80. While chatting to a new friend online, how would you describe the style of clothes that you are into?

81. Which day of the week is your most productive day? In what way?

82. Everyone in your family is pitching in on Saturday to clean the whole house and garage, and no one is pressuring you to join in. Would you help out or go to your friend's house? Why?

83. Is there an article of clothing you have that you just cannot do without? If so, what is it? Why is it so important?

84. In view of your diet, what is one food you try to eat regularly? Why?

85. Of everyone you know, who is the one person you feel you have the greatest responsibility toward? In what ways?

86. Would you find it easier to be totally, completely, 100% honest with your best friend or someone you're chatting with online? Why?

87. If you could write a different ending to one movie, which movie would it be? Why?

88.   When someone has a disagreement with you, how would you want him/her to handle it, for the best solution?

89.   Who are you most likely to compete with: someone who has less ability than you, someone whose ability is fairly equal to yours, or someone who has greater ability than you do? What would be an example?

90.   On a scale of 1 to 10, with 1 being total competition, and 10 being total cooperation, what number would you generally give yourself when working with people? When might this number change?

91.   Would you rather live in a city with a lot of cultural diversity, or a city where there is very little cultural diversity? Why?

92.   If you were going to design a T-shirt with a message, expressing your average Monday mood, what would your T-shirt say? Why?

93.   What is one way in which it is difficult for you to be more of an individual YOU?

94. Which collection of something you are keeping is the most valuable to you? In what way?

95. What is one song you would be very happy if you never heard again? Why?

96. What is the most unusual telephone call you have ever received? How did you respond? Why?

97. In reading the daily newspaper, which section do you usually check out first? Why?

98. When you are home sick, what are the items you usually need to help you pass the time comfortably? Why?

99. What are two things that make you really depressed when they happen, or when you think of them? Why?

100. On school days, what is your usual breakfast routine? Would you change it if you could? If so, how?

101. What is your favorite time of day? Why?

102. When you are in a park, what is your favorite thing to do? Why?

103. What is one of your favorite places to search on the Internet? Why?

104. What is the worst style of pizza you have ever eaten? Would you eat it again?

105. What is the best news that you have ever gotten in your life? What made it so outstanding?

106. When was the last time you were totally generous for absolutely no reason at all? What was the result?

107. What was the longest period of time you have stayed up and stayed awake? Would you do it again?

108. What can you just not get enough of when it comes to food?

109. When riding a motorcycle, would you voluntarily wear a helmet if it weren't required? Why, or why not?

—— if anybody asks me...

Growing Up

1. How do you know when you are grown up?

2. Would you rather live in a large city, or a small town? Why?

3. Who has it easier today - girls or boys? Why?

4. How would you feel if people continually mistook you for being two years younger than you are?

5. ...two years older?

6. What kind of work would you be willing to do if someone offered you $100? Why?

7. What is one thing that you really need (not want)?

8. What is one decision other people are making for you that you feel very capable of making? Why?

9. What is something you would pay $100 to be able to do? Why?

10. What is something you have seen others risk that you yourself would never do? Why?

11. Do you feel today's youth are getting a decent amount of respect from adults? Why, or why not?

12. When are the "good years" in a person's life?

13. What would you like to do to show others you're not a child any more? Why?

14. What rules do you have to follow that seem totally useless to you? Why?

15. For your 16th birthday present, you have a choice of getting your driver's license, a personal credit card, or a permanent backstage pass to your favorite rock group. Which would you choose? Why?

16. When should a child have the concept of death explained to them? Why?

17. What decisions should a person your age be allowed to make alone? Why?

18. What job would you not take $500 to do? Why?

19. What is the most enjoyable party you have ever attended? What made it so?

20. Should children be allowed to swear? If so, where? If not, then at what age?

21. What is a recent purchase you made with your own money that you now regret having made? Why?

22. What is a decision you made once that surprised everyone? Why?

23. Who is the last person to have sent you a thank-you note? For what reason?

24. Who could you send a thank-you note to? For what reason?

25. At what age should children be legally allowed to drive? Why?

26. What age is considered "old"? Why?

27. What makes a town or city a good place in which to live? Why?

28. What is a childhood toy you will probably never outgrow? Why?

29. How best could a child learn about sexuality? At what age?

30. When was a time you probably should have paid for something, but didn't? Why?

31. What day, or part of day, is the most boring part of the week for you? Why?

32. Would you be a different kind of person if you were given everything you simply wanted? Why, or why not?

33. If there were a pill to make you become gradually younger and younger, would you take it? Why, or why not? If so, at what age?

34. How important is it to you to have a good relationship with your friends' parents? Why, or why not?

35. What is a subject people think you should "lighten up" about? Why?

36. What is the most money you have ever made? Would you do it again?

37. What is the worst thing you ever cooked?

38. The same story is told by a book and also a movie. Would you read the book or see the movie? Why?

39. What was the worst punishment you ever received? Did you deserve it? Why or why not?

40. Is it important that each child in the family be given equal attention by the adults? Why, or why not?

41. When do you usually get yourself into trouble? Why?

42. What is the most danger you have ever been in? Could you go through it again, if necessary?

43. At what age should a person be allowed to get a permanent tattoo? Why?

44. Do children have rights that adults do not have? Why?

45. At what age should a person be given a credit card for personal use? Why?

46. How old should a person be in order to open a personal checking account? Why?

47. Should teenagers practice manners, or are manners out of style today? Why?

48. In what type of situation is it most difficult to remember to be polite and kind? Why?

49. Who inspires you? In what way?

50. Who gets inspiration from you? In what way?

51. If you could show everyone a "brag photo" of you, what would you be doing in it? Would anyone be in it with you?

52. Is a "troublemaker" as a child destined to be a "troublemaker" as an adult? Why, or why not?

53. What is something you need more courage yet to try? How can you develop that courage?

54. What is the best way to work out a conflict with another person? How successful are you in trying this approach?

55. What is a "soul mate"? Do you have one? How can you tell?

56. Is it easier being a child or an adult in our society today? How can you tell?

57. Are there some movies that young people your age should not be allowed to see? Why?

58. Is it harder to live up to your own expectations or those of others? Why?

59. Is there a subject about which you can take teasing from one person, but not from another? Why?

60. What is something you know you should be doing daily, but end up doing only occasionally? Why?

61. Based on your experiences in life, finish this sentence: "Sticks and stones may break my bones, but words..."

62. Would it be easier for you to create a list of 10 things that make you happy, or things that make you "bummed out"? Why?

63. What is the longest you have ever gone without eating? What happened afterward?

64. When is the last time a group of people applauded for you? What was it about?

65. Do children learn best by being punished, or by being rewarded for their behaviors? How can you tell?

66. What is something you were told when you were young that you now do not believe? Why?

67. What is something you probably could have been arrested for, but never got caught? Would you do it again?

68. Considering the influence you have on younger children, would you say you are more of a positive role model, or a negative role model? How can you tell?

69. What is one toy every child should own? Why?

70. Are store clerks usually respectful to customers your age? How can you tell?

71. Assuming your next birthday could not be celebrated with a cake, what would you request as a substitute? Why?

72. When was a time you felt helpless while with a person in need?

73. Are there things shown on TV that young people your age should not see? Why, or why not?

74. Two nurses, one female and one male, are in the doctor's office ready to help you. Would it make a difference which one you work with? Why, or why not?

75. Is it alright for a teenager to get their own apartment? If so, at what age?

76. Is it ever okay to leave young children home alone? If so, under what circumstances?

77. At what age should it no longer be necessary to tell your parents where you are going when you leave the house? Why?

78. What age should one be before having a personal telephone line? A cell phone? Why?

79. Should teenagers be required to pay all expenses for their own telephone line/cell phone? Why, or why not?

80. Can one be too young to have a part of their body pierced? Why, or why not?

81. For a major personal problem, whose advice would you want most? Why that certain person?

82. What are some times that you really need your own space? Why?

83. Should teens with part-time jobs still be assigned chores around the house? Why, or why not?

84. Can someone your age be "pushed" into the adult world too soon? How can you tell?

85. If child labor laws did not exist as they presently do, would you choose to be in school or working at a job right now? Why?

86. Should parents know all of their children's friends? Why, or why not?

87. When you are a parent, how much should you know about your child's friends? Why, or why not?

88. What is the most important experience each child should have to prepare them for later life? Why?

89.   You can select one word to be printed on your car's license plate which will reflect your driving style and habits. Which word would you choose? Why?

90.   What was the last situation in which you got really angry? What was your response? Why?

91.   Is it generally easier for you to be polite and respectful to adults, or kids your age? Why?

92.   Can you be too young to wear contact lenses? How can you tell?

93.   Are you more comfortable spending time with people younger or older than you? Why?

94.   How well do you deal with deadlines for assignments and projects? Why, or why not?

95.   Do you need more or fewer events in your life right now? Why?

96.   What is the most money you have ever spent on gifts for one Christmas season? Would you do that again? Why, or why not?

97. Do you see your present age as more of an advantage or a problem for you right now? In what ways?

98. At what age is it appropriate for someone to stay out all night? Why, or why not?

99. If you could be a role model to others, who would be your target audience, and what— through your words or actions—would be your message? Why?

100. When you graduate from school, you're asked to paint an inspirational message to younger students on a hallway wall. What message would you write? Why?

101. How old do you feel you have to be before your opinion really counts? Why?

102. Does a role model always need to be of the same gender? Why, or why not?

103. In terms of today's youth, does it seem that boys or girls have more role models? How can you tell?

104.   If you were given a monthly clothing allowance, what would be the LEAST amount of money you could get by with each month? What would most all of it go for?

105.   What is a situation in which competition is not good or productive? Why?

106.   What was the first album—tape or CD— that you ever purchased? When was the last time you listened to it?

107.   What is the first movie you went to a theater to see? Would you want to see it again? Why, or why not?

108.   How do you know when to accept money for work you have done, and when not to?

109.   Is there someone who takes you for granted? If so, in what ways? How would you like to have them treat you? Why?

110.   Many adults do certain things—such as smoke, drink coffee, gamble, or drink alcohol—and claim the privilege of being "adult" in order to do it. What is one "adult privilege" you think you will never take up when you are older? Why?

111. Name a time when you were very glad to get back home? Why?

112. Are there times, even while you are around people, that you feel you are "invisible"? What is happening that brings on that feeling?

113. What is your greatest accomplishment in life so far? Are you proud of it? Why, or why not?

114. Can you be too old to swing on a swing? Why, or why not?

115. What does it mean to "be yourself"?

Parents & Family

1. Would you raise your children differently than the way you are being raised? If so, how?

2. What would be the hardest thing for you to replace if there was a disaster on your property? Why?

3. How important is it to you that all family members sit down at one time and eat together? Why?

4. In a room full of parents, what advice would you like to give them? Why?

5. What would you say is the topic of most all arguing between kids your age and their parents? Why?

6. What is the best way to teach a child the right way to behave? Why?

7. What is the most important characteristic of a good child? Why?

8. How should decisions be made in a family? Why?

9. Should all kids be given an allowance? Why, or why not?

10. Do parents owe anything to their children? If so, what?

11. Do children owe anything to their parents? If so, what?

12. What is the most ideal/appropriate age for someone to become a parent? Why?

13. What is the most important characteristic of a good parent? Why?

14. Which family member do you take after the most? In what way(s)?

15. What are two ways your family depends on you? Why?

16. At what age should kids no longer have a curfew? Why?

17. What could your family use a little more of? What could they use a little less of? Why?

18. What is a fair way for a child of divorce to exist with both parents? Why is this the best?

19. For you, what would be the ideal number of brothers and sisters in your family? Why?

20. Should there be "wife-only" and "husband-only" chores in a marriage? Why, or why not?

21. Should every married couple have children? Why, or why not?

22. Should kids be allowed to drink alcoholic beverages at home? Why, or why not? If so, under what conditions?

23. What is a subject your parents and you disagree on? Why?

24. What is a present family custom you think you will continue when you have a family? Why?

25. Who is "better off": a child with no brothers and sisters, or a child with many bothers and sisters? Why?

26. How would you feel if you were told that your family will have a new baby in a few months? Why?

27. Do you think the ideal position is the first, last, middle, or only child in the family? Why?

28. Instructions your parents give you might not always be easy to carry out. Is there ever a time when disobeying parents might seem to be the only choice you have? Why?

29. What is the most enjoyable holiday celebrated in your family? Why?

30. What is the least enjoyable holiday celebrated in your family? Why?

31. What word would you choose to best describe the cooperation between everyone in your family? Why?

32. What special meal in your family would you invite your friends over to sample? Why?

33. What one activity would you like to spend more time doing with your parents? Why? Why/ isn't there time now?

34. What family decisions do the kids not need to have a voice in? Why not?

35. What would your friends learn by looking into your refrigerator? Why?

36. Are your concerns and worries the same as those your parents had when they were your age? Why, or why not?

37. What are some things your parents worried about when they were your age? Why?

38. Your friend is writing a play about a family with many members living in one house. If you are in the play, which role would you choose to have? Why?

39. Should parents be concerned about the music their kids listen to? Why, or why not?

40. What should teenagers expect their parents to pay for? Why, or why not?

41. Should all family members participate in household chores? Why, or why not?

42. Should parents pay their kids to get good grades? Why, or why not?

43. What is something you want very much to hear from your parents? Why?

44. Should parents divide child-care duties equally between themselves? Why, or why not?

45. Is divorce always a bad thing? Why, or why not?

46. Do parents have different expectations for daughters than they do for sons? If so, how can you tell?

47. At what age are you too old to get a hug from your parents? Why, or why not?

48. Should children be disciplined in public? Why, or why not?

49. What is one thing for which your parents are proud of you? How can you tell?

50. What is your most effective technique for getting what you want at home?

51. Is it possible for two adults to stay married for over 50 years? Why, or why not? If so, what would it take?

52. Should parents pay for property damage or vandalism done by their teenager? Why, or why not?

53. When do your parents watch you the most closely? For what reason?

54. Who is the most physically fit person in your family? How can you tell?

55. When should kids have a say in the family decision-making? How much input should they have?

56. What are some advantages to living in a step family? Why?

57. Should siblings in a family always be treated equally? Why, or why not?

58. Do you think kids embarrass their parents more, or do parents embarrass their kids more? How can you tell?

59. Should adopted children always be given total information about their biological parents? Why, or why not?

60. Should a wife or mother be allowed to manage her own personal checking account and money? Why, or why not?

61. Will you teach your kids to eat everything on their plate? Why, or why not?

62. Many parents do not want to see their child fail in anything. How much failure by your child might be tolerable to you? Why?

63. At home, would you say you are more over-protected, or under-protected? In what ways?

64. What is a punishment given to you that just does not work? Why doesn't it?

65. Lawyers, teachers, and doctors are all required to further their educations in order to graduate with a degree that enables them to do their best at their full-time profession. Should adults wishing to be parents have to study and earn a degree so they know how to be the very best possible parent for their children? Why, or why not?

66. Who, in your family, listens to you the most? How can you tell?

67. What are two things parents learn from their kids? Have your own parents learned these things?

68. What is something you would really like to have explained by your parents? Why?

69. What is the difference between "spoiling" a child, and giving a child what they want?

70. Can a child be given everything they ask for, and not end up "spoiled"? Why, or why not?

71. Your family is planning to attend the upcoming family reunion with all your relatives. Are you likely to go, or to try to talk your way out of going? Why?

72. Who, in your family, deserves more attention than they are getting now? In what way?

73. Do fathers have different expectations for their kids than mothers? If so, in what ways?

74. If you were promised one full hour of your parent's complete attention, how would you spend it? Why?

75. At what age should a child have explained to them that they are adopted? Why?

76. Are there any good reasons for a child to run away from home? Why, or why not?

77. At what age should kids be required to use their own money for personal items, rather than relying on their parents? Why?

78. What is the way that you can best show your parents that you can handle grown-up responsibility? How often do you?

79. You observe someone your age being yelled at and punished in a store by their parents. What would your reaction be? Why?

80. When, if at all, is it alright for an adult to act "childlike"? Why, or why not?

81. Who, in your family, gets more attention than they really need? How can you tell?

82. Which person in your family has the most strange sense of humor? In what way?

83. What is one way you would like to be more like your parents? Why?

84. What are two ways you want your children to take after you? Why?

85. Is it better for parents to allow their kids to experience life's hardships, or to shelter and protect them from all adult problems? Why?

86. Years from now, your child will ask to be left home alone for the weekend. What things should you, as a parent, consider before you do, or don't, give your child permission? Why?

87. Do you see yourself doing a lot, or very little, reading to your child someday? Why?

88. Do parents today need to be more or less strict with their kids? Why?

89. Your parents allow you to choose and rent one movie for the weekend. Is there any kind of movie that should not be brought home? If so, what kind is that?

90. When was the last time your parents told you that they are proud of you? Do you need to hear it more often?

91. How often should kids be told "I love you" by their parents? Why?

92. At home, do you have too little or too much freedom? Would you wish that to change? Why, or why not?

93. It seems to you that all your friends get a clothing allowance from their parents. Realizing this, how would you respond? Why?

94. Suppose that someday your teenager gets their license and begins driving the family car. Are there any expenses you would expect them to help with? Why, or why not?

95. Do your parents have a fairly accurate idea of what your friends are like, or would they be surprised if they knew more about your friends?

96. Are you more likely to enjoy your parents favorite style of music, or are they more likely to enjoy yours? Why?

97. As a parent, will you want a relationship with your kids in which they always tell you everything? Why, or why not? If not, where do you draw the line at what they shouldn't tell you?

98. Should kids be around when their parents are arguing, or should the parents save their fighting for a more private time, away from the kids? Why?

99.   Would your eating habits change in any way if you were always responsible for preparing your own meals at home? Why, or why not? If so, in what ways?

100.   How can you tell that you are in a good family?

101.   Should parents be 100% truthful with their kids, or are little "white lies" acceptable in order to get kids to behave or believe a certain way? Why?

102.   Does it get easier or harder to talk with your parents as you get older? Why do you suppose that is?

103.   Years from now, as a parent, you may be concerned about the TV shows your kids can watch. How would you best insure your kids will not see inappropriate shows? Why?

104.   What are two ways you would not punish your own children? Why?

105.   A new friend stays over with you at your house for the weekend. What would they learn about your family?

106. What book have you read that, when you are a parent, you will want to make sure your child reads? Why?

107. Is it necessary for single adults to set a goal of marriage for their future life? Why, or why not?

108. Your friend's parents own and play most all the current Top 10 CDs, including hip-hop, rap, and heavy metal. If you were their kid, would you be more pleased or embarrassed? Why?

109. How important is it for each kid in a family to receive equal attention from the adults? Why?

Friends & Peers —

1. Does it get easier or more difficult to make friends as you get older? Why?

2. How many friends is too many? Why?

3. Can you have too many friends? Why, or why not?

4. What is one thing about which you and your best friend disagree? Why?

5. If your best friend were to move away, what personal item would you like them to leave you? Why?

6. If you had to move, what personal item would you like to leave your best friend? Why?

7. A foreign student visiting you asks what American kids your age are like. What do you say? Why?

8. What one person your age do you think everyone should have a chance to get to know? Why?

9. When is peer pressure okay? Why?

10. What is something you want very much to hear from your friends? Why?

11. How much of what people say behind your back would you want to hear? Why?

12. What is a valuable lesson you have learned from one of your friends?

13. Do you get more privileges than your friends do? How can you tell?

14. Do today's teenagers do enough reading? How can you tell?

15. Are you more comfortable around someone who "has all the answers," or someone who will listen to other people's ideas? Why?

16. What makes someone popular? Why?

17. Can anyone be popular? Why, or why not?

18. If you could switch places with a friend in order to live with his/her family for one week, who would you choose? Why?

19. Who influences most of your daily decisions—males or females? In what way?

20. What is the most unlikely friendship you have ever made with someone? What made it so unusual?

21. What is something that you wish your friends understood better about you? Why?

22. What is something that gets in the way of your having more friends than you have right now? How could that change?

23. Who would you guess would like the chance to trade places with you for a week? Why?

24. Could you keep a secret from your current best friend? Why, or why not?

25. How does your own sense of humor compare with that of your present friends?

26. Could you tell your current best friend your most deep, private secret? Why, or why not?

27. In what way would you probably learn the most about someone—knowing what music they listen to, who they have as friends, or what their bedroom is like? Why?

28. Is your friend more likely to help you study for a test, or are you more likely to help them study for one? Why?

29. You have a chance to write to a special celebrity, requesting them to send a birthday greeting to your best friend. Which celebrity would your friend be most impressed with? Why?

30. Who is generally more critical of you—your friends or yourself? In what ways?

31. A longtime friend of yours begins making bad decisions, which have resulted in their suspension from school and a court appearance. Would you feel any responsibility to help your friend begin making better decisions? Why, or why not?

32. What type of person is it most difficult for you to be friends with? Why?

33. Your best friend is asked to confide the most private secret you've shared with them to someone else. Would your best friend tell, or not? Why?

34. Where is a good place to go if you want to make new friends? Why?

35. Do you choose friends immediately, or take time to judge people? Why?

36.   Is it easy or diffic[...]

37.   Are you pleased w[...]
have right now among y[...]
you wish it coul[...]

38.   Are you able to tell your [...] ...u wnat you
don't like about them? Why, or why not?

39.   What is the best way your friends can help
out when you are angry? Why?

40.   What is the best way your friends can help
out when you are depressed? Why?

41.   How would you define a "clique"?

42.   Most schools have "cliques." Is a clique
different than a group of people?

43.   Is it considered "cool" to be in a clique at
your school? Why, or why not?

44.   Is belonging to the "right" group in school
important to you? Why, or why not?

45.   Have you ever found yourself a part of the
wrong group at school? If so, what did you
do?

...ing a new friend, how important to
...u is what other friends say about that
person? Why, or why not?

47. If you had no money to spend on a birthday
    gift for your best friend, what would you do
    to help them have a memorable celebration?
    Why?

48. Your best friend has been down in the dumps
    for a long time. What movie would you
    recommend to help them get back to feeling
    normal? Why?

49. Your best friend and you get along real
    well when you are by yourselves, but in the
    group, the same friend as much as pretends
    you don't exist. What would you do? Why?

50. Is it possible for someone to "outclass"
    themselves—work so hard to be "at the
    top" that other people will feel this actually
    normal, average person isn't reachable?
    What can happen?

51. Who do you think has more embarrassing
    moments—guys or girls? How can you tell?

52. You find out from another person that your best friend tells his/her parents EVERYTHING. Would this affect your relationship with that person at all? Why, or why not? If so, in what ways?

53. When sharing a candy bar with your friend, are you likely to give him/her the biggest piece? Why, or why not?

54. How would you describe the "perfect" friend? Why? How close do you come to this description?

55. A friend in your close group is continually swearing, even at your home. Would it offend you? What, if anything, would you do about it? Why, or why not?

56. What is the one characteristic that you feel most all of your friends respect you for?

57. Do you have one close friend, or many friends? Would you wish that to change in any way?

58. A good friend of yours is in many school groups, joins other kids after school almost daily, and is frequently asked for advice by others. Yet this same person confides to you that they are worried that they don't have any friends. Could they be right? What would you say to them?

Relationships —

1. What advice would you give someone your age who has trouble making friends? Why?

2. Who is the person you trust the most? How much do you trust them?

3. What is something kind that someone has done for you recently?

4. Are you closer to your parents or your friends right now? Why?

5. How can someone know they are being given respect by another person?

6. Is it okay to lie to someone if they have lied to you?

7. Is it okay to cheat someone if they have cheated you?

8. When is revenge okay?

9. Who is the person you feel the most comfortable around? Why?

10. Who would you like to have a better relationship with right now? In what way?

11. Could you go 24 hours being totally honest? Why, or why not?

12. Who can you be totally honest with? How do you know?

13. Can you be more honest with an adult, someone your own age, or a child? Why?

14. Who is the person you admire the most? For what reasons?

15. What quality is most important to you in choosing a friend? Why?

16. Does one person deserve more respect than another? Who? Why?

17. What is a quality of yours you wish people would recognize in you more often?

18. Who is someone you can always count on for help? In what way?

19. What is a good way for you to tell a friend you don't want to be with them any longer?

20. Who is someone who has learned a lot from you? What have they learned?

21. Can any good be accomplished by two or more people arguing? If so, what?

22. Is there anyone whose nerves you get on occasionally? If so, how?

23. Who is likely to say the kindest things about you most any time?

24. Who are you most likely to share good news with first? Why?

25. Who are you most likely to share bad news with first? Why?

26. Who should be the person to apologize first in an argument? Why?

27. When is the last time you said "I'm sorry" to someone?

28. What quality in a person generally gets them respect from others—height, attitude, talent, or something else? Why?

29. Should girls be allowed in the Boy Scouts? Why, or why not?

30. Should boys be allowed in the Girl Scouts? Why, or why not?

31. Should women be able to take up boxing with men? Why, or why not?

32. Should males wear makeup and color their nails as females do? Why, or why not?

33. Would you ever want someone to lie to you? If so, when?

34. Who is someone you would never "let down"? Why not?

35. Who is someone you recently helped feel better? How?

36. What is the nicest compliment you've ever been given? Did you agree with it?

37. What is a compliment given to you that took you by surprise? Why?

38. Who is someone that can always depend on you? In what way?

39. Who is the person that knows the most about you, inside and out?

40. When was a time you were truly frightened for someone else?

41. When do you tend to be a leader more than a follower? Why?

42. When do you tend to be a follower more than a leader? Why?

43. Who are the better care-givers; males or females? Why?

44. Should both genders be allowed to play on the same high school sports teams, or should there be separate teams? Why?

45. If you could not talk, how would you choose to communicate with others? Why?

46. Who, generally, is more competitive—males or females? How can you tell?

47. Are guys just as capable of efficient baby-sitting as girls? Why, or why not?

48. Are there any sports that should truly be for only one gender? Why, or why not?

49. A male friend a few years older than you explains that he has almost decided about training to be a nurse, and wants your honest opinion. What do you tell him? Why?

50. Is it better to trust too much, or too little?
    Why?

51. Who do you wish you could be more open
    and honest with? What makes it difficult?

52. Who has seen all of your moods?

53. Is it easier for males or females to adapt to
    non-traditional gender-related activities?
    Why?

54. Is it possible to be in a crowd of several
    hundred people, and still be "alone"? Why,
    or why not?

55. Are you more likely to spend most of your
    time with your trusted and true friends, or
    search out new friendships in new places?
    Why?

56. What is the most necessary characteristic
    to make a relationship last between two
    people? Why is that important?

57. What would you do to get involved at a party
    where you know almost no one? Why?

58.   Some people in your class are putting down a new student who you have found to be very interesting and nice. What would you do? Why, or why not?

59.   When is an age difference between people not important? Why not?

60.   What is one generalization, or stereotype, about people that you intensely disagree with? Why does it seem so inaccurate?

61.   When it comes to anger, who handles it more appropriately—females or males? How can you tell?

62.   Was there ever a time when you knew you were right about something, when everyone around you was convinced that you were wrong? If so, what was the situation? What did you learned from it?

63.   How would you describe "discrimination"? Do you ever see examples of discrimination at your school?

64.   Is there a "weaker sex"? How can you tell?

65. Should all jobs be equally available to both men and women, or are some jobs meant for one gender only? Why?

66. Is it more important for you to feel accepted, or feel popular, at school? What is the difference?

67. At what age should one be allowed to date? Should this be the same for both genders?

68. Should a girl ask a guy out on a date? Why, or why not?

69. Should a guy pay all the expenses on a date? Why, or why not?

70. Would it be okay for your best friend to date your ex? Why, or why not?

71. Which person in the couple should buy the tickets to their prom? Why?

72. Is it okay for adolescents of different races to date each other? Why, or why not?

73. What would be some signs that the person you're "going with" and you are "drifting apart"?

74. What is the most important characteristic for a girlfriend or a boyfriend? Why?

75. Are the initial fears about going out "on a date" the same for a girl as they are for a guy? Why, or why not?

76. Is "going together" the same as "dating"? If not, what is the difference?

77. What is the most acceptable and proper way for your partner to break up with you? Why?

78. When an engagement for marriage is broken, should the engagement ring be returned to the buyer? Why, or why not?

79. At the end of a relationship, would you be more likely to save and treasure the souvenirs from your ex, or throw out everything that reminds you of them? Why?

80. You have the opportunity to go out with one of three people; the first is attractive, the second has personal charm, and the third is intelligent. Whom would you choose? Why?

81. Three different people want to go on a date with you; the first because of your personality, the second because of your personal charm, and the third because of your intelligence. Which would you choose? Why?

82. In choosing a partner for marriage, do you think that "opposites attract," or do the two people need to be extremely similar in attitudes and interests? Why?

83. Does an age difference between two people dating each other really make a difference? Why, or why not?

84. Will you need your future spouse to be a member of the same religion as you are? Why, or why not?

85. In a relationship, how honest do you want your partner to be? Why?

86. After meeting a new person, your close friend asks you how you know when you are in love. What do you say? Why?

87. Is personal safety while on a date a concern among you and your friends? Why, or why not?

88.   Your best friend tells you that their parents don't like the person they are going out with, and would not mind seeing the two "split up." Being best friends, they ask your advice. How would you respond? Why?

89.   Can someone be too young to be in a romantic relationship? How can you tell?

90.   Your best friend and you have just begun reading the questions in the book "Answers for the Perfect Relationship." What question would you most want the answer to? Why?

91.   Should a husband and wife work to be 100% truthful with each other, or is it okay to keep some secrets from your partner? Why, or why not?

92.   Should all marriages be bound by a "prenuptial agreement," a contract accepted and signed by both the bride and groom. Why, or why not?

93.   Before they marry each other, is it important for a husband and wife to know all about each others' past? Why, or why not? If not, how much should be known?

94. Many married couples from past generations have been married for 50 years and longer. Does that length of time seem realistic for today's youth? Why, or why not?

95. What is your most important rule or piece of advice for a successful date? Why?

96. The person you are dating, as well as your best friend, are both complaining that you spend too much time with the other person, and not enough time with them. How would you resolve this issue between the three of you? Why?

97. Finding yourself in the middle of a dispute with the person you are dating and your best friend, would your faithfulness and loyalty stay equally divided between them, or would you be more steadfast and true to one of them? Why?

Teen Angst

1. Most of your friends, it seems, have some body part pierced, and are encouraging you to do it, also. Your parents have repeatedly said they do not want you to do this, but they are not always around. What would you do? Why?

2. You've been grounded—stay at home, no visitors—for the next four weeks. Your group of friends pressures you about your turn to host the next party. One friend suggests this next weekend, aware that your parents will be out of town. What would you decide? Why?

3. Your younger brother wants you to drive him about 10 miles to his friend's house. Your own friend, with you at the time, encourages you to do it, not knowing that, legally, you still need an adult with you. No one else will find out. What would you decide? Why?

4. Your good friend has the position you want on the team. Smoking is against team policy. Knowing he/she smokes, would you tell to get the position? Why, or why not?

5. What is a difficult decision you have had to deal with lately? What made it difficult?

6. What do you do when you are angry? Why?

7.   Would you wear fashionable shoes or clothes even if they were uncomfortable? Why, or why not?

8.   What would you do if you found out today that you were going to move? Why?

9.   Is it okay to break a promise? If so, when?

10.   A classmate tries to slip you some answers to a test you didn't study for. What would you do? Why?

11.   What kind of clothes put you in a good mood? Why?

12.   Is there someone who pries into your life too much? How? Why?

13.   What importance does a movie's rating have on whether or not you will go to it? Why?

14.   A good friend encourages you to drop a CD in your bag. The store clerk is in the back room. What would you do? Why?

15.   You find out that a friend of yours has stolen something from another friend of yours. What would you do? Why?

16. What are the most common reasons for someone your age to get into trouble?

17. What would make life easier for someone your age? Why?

18. What is something you think is incredibly expensive right now? What price would be more reasonable? Why?

19. Would you ever lie to protect a friend? Why, or why not?

20. What is a time you should have said something, but didn't? Why not?

21. What is a lie that's been told about you? Why?

22. Your best friend wants to drop out of school right now to get a full-time job. What would you tell them? Why?

23. Your friend tells you that cheer leading is not a real sport. Would you agree or disagree with them? Why?

24. If you found someone's credit card lying on the ground, what would you do? Why?

25. Is embarrassment always a bad thing? Why, or why not?

26. You are a baby-sitter. Would you work at a house where the parents video tape what you and the children do? Why, or why not?

27. Your friend suggests the two of you take a few cans of spray paint and use them on an old, empty house. What would you say? Why?

28. Your best friend wants to stay at a party, where a few kids are doing things you personally don't like. What would you do? Why?

29. As a student representative to your town's city council, you can cast the deciding vote on whether your town will build a new stadium, a library, or a shopping mall. Which would you choose? Why?

30. How do you decide whether something is right or wrong?

31. Is it easier for you to deal with criticism from a friend, or from your parents? Why?

32. Is there someone who makes you feel that you're not "good enough" for them? How do they do that?

33. Should the truth always be told, or should some things be left unexplained? Why?

34. Your best friend has recently begun drinking at home and is throwing a party this weekend. Most of your friends are going. What would you do? Why?

35. What is your usual reaction when you become depressed? Why?

36. When you become "stressed out," how do you usually respond? Why?

37. What is a "burning question" you really wish you had the answer to, right now? Why?

38. Your town's leaders come to you wanting some ideas on how to attract more tourists and visitors to the area. What would you tell them? Why?

39. Is there a situation you are aware of that you hope nobody ever finds out about? Why?

40. What usually brings on your most uncomfortable, terrible headaches?

41. Who is the one person you would most likely talk to when a family crisis occurs? Why?

42. While chatting on the Internet, a new person of the opposite sex asks you to describe how you look. Are you more likely to describe yourself accurately, or to stretch the truth a little? Why?

43. Tonight, you have to choose between baby-sitting and earning some outstanding, necessary money, or going out with friends for one last summer fling. What would you do? Why?

44. Your grandparents will supply money for your whole back-to-school wardrobe. Your parents tell you to go cheap. How much would you ask for? Why?

45. You are the only one in your crowd without a date for the dance. What would you do? Why?

46. What is the most important factor—price, style, brand name, etc.—in determining which gym shoes to buy? Why?

47. A good friend dares you to get a permanent tattoo on a place no one will ever see. What would you do? Why?

48.   You have a chance to set a school record tonight at the swim meet for all-time number of 1st place ribbons, but you are feeling very ill. Your substitute, if you let them take your place, is also likely to win a ribbon, which they have never yet done. The decision is yours. What would you do? Why?

49.   At a school track meet you have an opportunity to set a new personal record or help your team set a new team record, but you can't enter both events. Which would you choose to do? Why?

50.   You are upset by the fact that a friend of yours is taking drugs. Your friend's parents ask if you know anything about your friend's unusual behavior. What would you do? Why?

51.   For your next science project, you must choose between pairing up with your best friend, who has absolutely no study skills or desires, or with the class "geek", who you know could help you earn an easy "A." Which would you choose? Why?

52.   Do adults generally understand the problems your friends and you deal with each day? How can you tell?

53. What is a pressure you would like to be relieved of, right now? Why?

54. Your best friend comes to school in a 'doo' that you know will be made fun of for the next week. What do you do? Why?

55. When is cheating not really cheating? Why not?

56. When does bad language seem acceptable or appropriate? Why, or why not?

57. A few students are able to get excellent grades while participating in sports, and working at a part-time job. Could you do all three? Rank them in order of their importance to you.

58. Before the game, you see your teammate privately take a pill, and seeing you, say that it's only for the pain. Would you be concerned at all? Why, or why not?

59. You have a ten-page report due Monday, which you haven't started. Your close friends have invited you on a camp out over the weekend. What would you do? Why?

60.   On a trip with your friends, each person has brought their own kind of music. Since everyone has their own favorite style, how do you insure that no one's feelings will be hurt? Is this possible?

61.   Can—or should—gossip be controlled? Why, or why not?

62.   You become aware that there is talk about you going around at school. How does this make you feel? Why?

63.   What are some reasons why it is hard for teens to talk openly with their parents?

64.   How do you know when you have too many clothes?

65.   What type of clothing would you not be "caught dead" in? Why?

66.   One of your friends often forks over their homework for others to use, and also doesn't cover up their test answers. A close friend of yours is bothered by that, and wants to know what you think. What would you tell them? Why?

67. Do you hear more negative stories or positive stories about what today's teenagers do? Why do you suppose that is?

68. Your friend has told you that his teammates all decided to shave their heads for the season, and never asked him about the idea, which he doesn't agree with. How would you advise him? Why?

69. Your good friend tells you that they are frequently abused at home, and then asks you to never say a word to anyone. What would you do? Why?

70. While you are in a department store with your friends, one of them takes something off the shelf, puts it into their pocket, and proceeds to walk out of the store unseen by anyone else, leaving the rest of you. What would you do? How would you feel about that happening? Why?

71. Eyebrow piercing is getting popular with the in-crowd at your school; it seems the only people getting respect are the ones getting something pierced. Would you choose to follow suit and get yours pierced? Why, or why not?

72. Is it bad to be labeled a "wannabe"? Why, or why not?

73. Your parents have decided that the family can do without a telephone for a number of reasons. How would you respond? Why?

74. Your crowd is becoming more exercise-conscious and plans major workouts more times each week. Would you join them? Why, or why not?

75. You feel you are losing your best friend, who is suddenly joining the in-crowd at school. What would you do? Why?

76. Your parents are going to be gone for the weekend and instuct you not to invite any friends over. Would you? Why, or why not?

77. How do you know when a party you are attending is getting out of hand? Would you leave it? Why, or why not?

78. You know the college that your best friend is planning to attend, and you want desperately to go with them. However, you have just been awarded a full scholarship to a different college. What would you do? Why?

79. At home, is it a problem getting enough privacy for your telephone calls? Why, or why not?

80. Are you more likely to wear "trendy" clothes, or all-purpose, anytime clothes? Why?

81. A friend in your group has owed you $10 for months. Are you more likely to remind them about the money, or just let it pass in the name of friendship? Why?

82. While you are taking a test you didn't study at all for, your teacher goes to the office. What would you do? Why, or why not?

83. Your good friend calls and asks you over for the night, not knowing that you have been invited to a major party at which he/she would not be welcome. What would you do? Why, or why not?

84. The only seat left in the crowded lunch room is at the table with the kids nobody generally sits with. What would you do? Why?

85. Looking younger than your age, would you purposely try to get into a movie at a cheaper price? Why, or why not?

86.   A friend of yours who you know has a difficult home life is planning to run away. How involved would you get with their decision? Why, or why not?

87.   Your friend is worried about losing the 20 pounds in ten days that both he and the coach want gone for the lower weight class. How would you respond to your friend? Why?

88.   To decrease the number of teen driving accidents, many states are adopting the "Graduated Licensing" law, which puts more restrictions on getting a full license, slowing down the process for teens to drive independently.   Does this seem a reasonable, effective law? Why, or why not?

89.   What kind of party would you not consider attending? Why not?

90.   The party you are hosting is "crashed" by a group of unknown teens. What would you do? Why, or why not?

91.   Your principal has just received tickets to the Final Four college basketball championship for two students in your school. What is the best way to give the tickets out? Why?

92. While you are at your friend's house, their brother complains that he's going to be late for the school program. Because your friend cannot drive the car, they ask you to drive their family car to take the brother to school. What would you do? Why, or why not?

93. Your close friend is not a good driver, and you are uncomfortable about being in the car while they are driving, even though they seem to be the "taxi driver" for most all of your group's activities. How would you deal with your concerns? Why?

94. After a new friend has visited your house several times, you suspect that he/she has taken a few small—but not cheap—items that belonged to your parents. How would you handle this situation? Would you handle it differently if it involved a long-time friend? Why, or why not?

95. When you get home with your new pair of jeans, you check the receipt and find that you were overcharged $2. What would you do? Why, or why not? Would you shop at that store again?

96. At school, both candidates for class president personally ask for your vote. One is your longtime, good friend who doesn't have a clue about organization or keeping promises. The other is someone you don't personally get along with, but you know this person is intelligent and talented at whatever they try. Who would you vote for? Why?

97. One night, home alone, you receive an uncomfortable phone call from someone you don't know. You do not have access to Caller ID. What would you do? Why, or why not?

98. On checking your receipt as you walk out of the music store, you find you were charged $2 less for your CD than you should have been. What do you do? Why, or why not? If you were the clerk, what would you want a customer to do?

99. While driving alone, you back into and dent, another person's car. No one else is around. What would you do? Why, or why not?

100. Driving alone at night, your car breaks down. A car stops and the driver offers to take you to the next town. What do you do? Why? What are your alternatives?

101. You attend a party without your parent's permission. The only person you know is your good friend who drove you both. During the party, your friend becomes drunk. What do you do? Why?

102. While you are shopping for clothes with your group, you notice that one of your friends is in the process of changing tags on a pair of jeans, in order to pay a lower price. What would you do? Why, or why not?

103. The person at a table next to you gets up and, as they leave, you see a $5 bill drop from his/her pocket. What would you do? Why, or why not?

104. You have the perfect part-time job, giving you needed money, and yet enough free time for school sports, church activities, hanging with friends, and homework. Your boss just sold the store to another person, who wants you to work twice as many hours. As jobs are hard to come by, what would you do? Why, or why not?

105. You have the choice of two, would pay below-average wages, would be doing work you greatly enjoy other would pay fantastic wages but the work is definitely not something you want to do. Which would you choose? Why?

106. One day your good friend asks you to recommend him/her to your boss for a position which would allow you to work together. However, you feel your friend would not be good at this job, which could reflect on you. What would you do? Why?

107. At a football game, the ticket clerk walks away temporarily and does not see you at the gate waiting to buy a ticket. Would you wait for them, or go through without paying? Why?

108. You were asked to research and write an original report. A classmate tells you that he/she downloaded a paper on the topic, asking you not to say anything. Later, the teacher asks if you have heard anything about this same student not writing an original report. What would you do? Why, or why not?

109. The restaurant you and your friends go to is full, except for a few seats in the "Smoking" section. Your friends want to stay, not knowing your discomfort around smoke. What would you do? Why?

110. On the day report cards are delivered through the mail, you receive not only yours but another student's card whose last name is the same as yours. Knowing you could fix it so no one would ever notice, would you check out his/her grades before returning it? Why, or why not?

111. What, to you, would be an acceptable reason for returning your meal to the kitchen at the restaurant? Have you ever done that?

112. You invite a friend to sleep-over. When you return to the bedroom with snacks, you find that your friend has turned on the kind of movie that you are not allowed to watch. What would you do? Why, or why not?

113. A classmate has found the answers to a semester test, and is passing them out to most of the other students. How would you react to this problem? Why, or why not?

114.   A shy, but extremely intelligent student you do not particularly like has teamed up with your close, but not too bright, friend on the latest science project. After their class presentation, it's clear that the teacher thinks your friend did most of the work, and therefore, gives your friend most of the credit. You, however, know that your friend did nothing more on the project than present it to the class. What would your reaction be? Why?

115.   A close friend of yours tells you that, after she graduates, she is going to be a fashion model, and she needs to lose at least 15 pounds. This surprises you, since your friend is already on the thin side. How would you respond to her? Why?

116.   Although you work to stay in the best fashions like your closest friends, the latest trend in clothing is way beyond your price range. What would you do? Why?

117. A music store is giving away dozens of single-song CDs from a variety of singers and groups. The CDs are left unattended in a large box with a sign next to them that says, "One to a customer, please." With no one else around, what would you do? Why?

118. The really tight group you are in decides to kick the meat habit and become vegetarians. You are not ready to give up your rights to beef. What would you do? Why?

119. Your one wish is to play for a big-name university, but a lesser-known college has just offered you a full four-year scholarship to play for them and promised you playing time. What would you decide? Why?

School

1. If it weren't for school, what do you think you would you be doing? Why?

2. Describe how you know you are in a good school.

3. What is the most valuable way you can help your school? Why?

4. In what way do you hope this will be a better year? How can you help make it happen?

5. How would it be to have year-round school? Why?

6. How much authority should students have in setting school policies? Why?

7. Your school has a suggestion box. What idea(s) would you write to make your school a better place? Why?

8. How would you feel about being MC of a program in front of all the students and teachers? Why?

9. What's your opinion about male cheerleaders in high school? Why, or why not?

10. What school subject would you rather study without a textbook? Why?

11. All the students stand, clap and cheer one day when you enter the room. How would you feel? Why?

12. Who gets more respect at your school—females or males? How can you tell?

13. Should high school students be required to do community service before they graduate? Why, or why not?

14. Should PE be a requirement in school? Why, or why not?

15. When is it appropriate to share your homework? Why?

16. Some public schools run male-only and female-only classes. If you had the chance, would you go to a school like this? Why, or why not?

17. How do students at your school treat other students who are "different"? Do you approve of this treatment? Why, or why not?

18. Do you see high school graduation more as the "end" or the "beginning" for you? In what way?

19. A student can legally drop out of high school any time after 16 years of age. Is this law reasonable, or should every student be required to complete 12 grades? Why?

20. If you were on your school's Student Council, how motivational do you think you could be to the rest of the students? Why?

21. Would you rather attend a large school with hundreds of students, or a smaller school of about two hundred? Why?

22. The Board of Education in your town asks your opinion about making the school day longer for all students. What would you tell them? Why?

23. When your teacher and parents disagree on something, who do you usually tend to side with? Why?

24. Other than actually being ill, what would be a reason important enough for you to call in "sick" to school? Has this ever happened?

25. Considering your worst memory of school so far, how well could you live through that if it happened again? Why?

26. Should school officials be able to check out student lockers? Why, or why not? If so, under what conditions?

27. Should a very above-average student be allowed to move ahead a grade or two? Why, or why not?

28. You are an exceptionally gifted student. Assuming it was your own choice, would you want to move ahead a grade or two? Why, or why not?

29. Your school asks for suggestions on how to make the library more valuable to students. What suggestion would you give? Why?

30. Most students do not like school-prepared lunches. What ideas would you have for making lunches more popular, affordable, and at the same time, still as nutritious as possible?

31. What is the most effective technique you use in studying for a test?

32. How much of a friend do you think teachers should be with their students? Why?

33. Do teachers in your school handle discipline problems well, or could it be done more effectively? How?

34. If you were a teacher, how would you keep students your age interested in learning?

35. As a school principal, you become aware that several students are getting permanent tattoos, resulting in a great deal of extra attention from their peers. How would you react? Why?

36. What is the worst test you have ever had in school? What made it that way?

37. What type of student in your school seems to get the most respect from peers? How can you tell?

38. If your school could win the state championship in one sport, which sport would you want it to be? Why?

39. Should there be any consequences for a student found smoking at school? Why, or why not?

40. Many schools have a "no hat" policy in their buildings. Is this a good policy, or not? Why?

41. At school, what is the most comfortable room for you to be in? Why?

42. While you are at school, what is your greatest worry or concern? Why?

43. You hear that your school staff is considering requiring all students to wear uniforms. They say it will help build unity and cut down on discipline problems. What would you say? Why?

44. What are some good things about going to a new school?

45. What style of clothing would not be "cool" at your school? Why not?

46. Which school subject seems the most pointless to you? In what ways?

47. Which school subject seems the most valuable to you? In what ways?

48. If you could make one change in your school's dress code, what would that be? Why?

49. If you wrote the school policy, would there be any consequences for students not attending classes? If so, what would you recommend? Why?

50. Your principal wants your input on the school's attendance policy. How would you make it fair and appropriate for all students?

51. Should students be allowed to retake a test as many times as necessary in order to finally pass it? Why, or why not?

52. How many people know your locker combination? How safe do you feel with that?

53. Do teachers have any responsibility to students who fail their tests? If so, what are those responsibilities?

54. How much homework is too much? How can you tell?

55. A new school will be grouping their students for classes by ability level in each subject rather than by age. If you had a choice, would you go to this school? Why, or why not?

56. What can someone in your school do to become popular? Why is that effective?

57. Are there any advantages for students who go to an all-boy's or an all-girl's school? Why, or why not? If so, what are some?

58. What new student activities could your school include to make it a more interesting place? Why?

59. In your school, are girls given the opportunity to be seen as equally smart as boys? Why, or why not?

60. A girl at your school wants to go out for wrestling. How do you think most other students will react to the news? Why?

61. In your school, is it important for students to be aware of cultural and ethnic differences? Why, or why not?

62. Should high schools require a class on effective parenting techniques before graduation? Why, or why not?

63. Large class size is a problem in many schools. What would you say is the perfect number of students for a class? Why?

64. What would you do if you got to school and realized that the very important take-home math test was left at home? Why?

65. Many people think history is an important subject to study. Would you agree? Why, or why not?

66. What is the best meal that your school serves? Which meal could definitely NOT be called their best? Why?

67. How do you know when you are sitting in the wrong place in the lunch room?

68. Do students in your classes treat each other with enough respect? How can you tell?

69. At the beginning of a new class, when you are allowed to sit in the desk of your choice, which desk are you most likely to take? Why?

70. At school, one group hangs together and tells each other all the secrets they have heard; another group gets together but, generally, keeps their secrets private and unmentioned. Which group would you feel most comfortable around? Why?

71. Suppose your school allowed you one day off to either follow a worker of your choice while they performed their job, or to visit a college campus of your choice. Which would you choose? Why? What would you hope to learn?

72. A new student, who cannot speak a word of English, joins your class. What would your behavior, or reaction be to this person? Why?

73. Is your school doing everything possible to prepare you for life after graduation? If not, what more would you suggest?

74. A certain movie would be perfect to explain the subject your class is studying in school; however, it has an "R" rating. Should it be allowed in class? Why, or why not?

Sports

1. When was the last time you purposely lost a game or contest? What was the reason?

2. What sport in the U.S. could be eliminated? Why?

3. Is it okay for sports fans to boo and heckle pro players? Why, or why not?

4. Is it okay for sports fans to boo and heckle high school athletes? Why, or why not?

5. Which sport should claim the title of "National Pastime"? Why?

6. Should there be a women's professional football conference? Why, or why not?

7. Do coaches have a right to yell and scream at referees? Why, or why not?

8. Is winning everything? Why, or why not?

9. If you could own one professional team, which one would it be? Why?

10. Is it more acceptable to be unsportsmanlike and win, or show good sportsmanship and lose? Why?

11. When is it okay to show unsportsmanlike behavior to win? Why?

12. Would you be satisfied with having done your best, even if you lost the game? Why, or why not?

13. Do you have to have played the sport in order to be a good coach? Why, or why not?

14. They could not pay you enough money to be a referee of what sport? Why not?

15. Which sports record is so special that it should never be broken? Why?

16. Would a professional women's baseball team be as popular as the men's teams? Why, or why not?

17. If perfect refereeing—done electronically— during games were possible, would you be in favor of it? Why, or why not?

18. Should an athlete play the position the coach needs and wants them in, or the position they want to play? Why?

19. What would it be like if serious, aggressive conflicts could be settled on the basketball court?

20. There are many substances that athletes use to increase their performance. As an athlete looking for improved performance, would you take a substance like this? Why, or why not?

21. Does a team from a large school have any advantages over a team from a smaller school? Why, or why not?

22. Which sport needs the most changes in its rules? Why?

23. In an extremely competitive game, are you more likely to play by the rules, or do "whatever it takes" to win? Why?

24. Athletes and fans are frequently becoming more abusive toward referees during games. How much disrespect should referees have to deal with during a game? Why?

25. In a championship tournament, which type of contest is most fair and accurate: teams playing 2-out-of-3 games, or a 1-time contest for a single winner? Why?

26. Would most sports change if scores were not kept during the game? If so, how?

27. Should some, all, or none of the athletes on college teams be paid? Why, or why not?

28. When is playing the team's best players more important than giving all players equal time? Why?

29. Is the final score always the most important part of a game? Why, or why not?

30. Is there something you, yourself, can personally learn when you lose a contest or game? If so, what?

31. As a referee, you make a call that is not correct. Would you want it to be immediately overturned by another referee in the interest of fairness, or should your first decision stand? Why?

32. If the goal of team competition is to beat the opposition, would this change in any way if members of both teams could meet each other either before or after the game? Why, or why not?

33. Some people say that the team that works the hardest will win. Do you agree? Why, or why not?

34. Are you satisfied with your school's academic requirements for participating in sports? Why, or why not?

35. One school's academic standards require no F's for participants of sports, while at another school, an athlete may remain eligible with 3 F's. Which set of standards is more helpful to students? Why?

36. Is it more the school's responsibility, or that of the parents, to set academic standards for kids who want to participate in school athletics? Why?

37. Should drug testing be routinely done for high school athletes? Why, or why not?

38. You are on a team where the coach regularly gets abusive with you and the other players. How much "negativity" would you take from a coach before quitting the team? Why, or why not?

39. While trying to motivate and encourage the athletes on a team, can a coach go too far in pushing for better performance? If so, in what ways?

40. To you, what is the main reason a person should go out for sports?

41. Would you feel you accomplished more after a basketball game if you had fouled out, or not fouled at all? Why?

42. If it were your choice, would you rather play in all of a junior varsity game, or "warm the bench" during most of the varsity game? Why?

43. Many people say there is truth in the phrase, "No pain, no gain". Do you agree with the idea of this saying? Why, or why not?

44. Should coaches' employment depend on their team's win/loss record? Why, or why not?

45. If you had the chance to be a member of the U.S. Olympic team for either the summer or winter games, in which sport would you choose to participate? Why?

46. Should professional athletes be allowed to continue as participants of Olympic teams, or should the teams include only amateur athletes? Why?

Past/Future

1. If you could have been born at an earlier time, what is one thing you would like to have experienced? Why?

2. How can you make today better than yesterday?

3. What is one chance you now wish you would have taken? Why?

4. If you packed only one of your possessions in a suitcase to use the rest of your life, what would it be? Why?

5. If you could become aware of your own future, would you want to? Why, or why not?

6. What is destiny? Do you have one?

7. What famous person from the past would you like to have a long conversation with? Why?

8. What one thing would you like to have named after you? Why?

9. What job will there be in 100 years that is non-existent now?

10. How will you know that you've got a good job or career?

11. What is one hour you would like to live over? Why?

12. What is one hour you would not like to live over? Why?

13. If you could make one decision over again, what would it be? Why?

14. If you lived 100 years from now, what kind of job do you think you would have? Why?

15. If you could take a pill giving you eternal life, would you? Why, or why not?

16. If you could not live in the present, would you choose the past or future instead? Why?

17. What do you see happening in the United States in the next 100 years? How can you tell?

18. How will houses be different in the future?

19. If you won $11 million while you had a job, would you continue working? Why, or why not?

20.   Which word do you hope will describe your life when you are older: rich, famous, or happy? Why?

21.   If you could put away one possession of yours for your grandchildren as an example of your childhood, what would you choose? Why?

22.   What saying would you want written on your tombstone? Why?

23.   What is your formula for being successful as an adult? Why?

24.   Would you rather work a daytime shift, or an evening shift? Why?

25.   Without being rich, how much money would you need to live comfortably? Why?

26.   If you could look into the future, what new sport would you see people playing in 100 years? Why?

27.   In what form—book, movie, park, etc.— would you want to leave people a lasting memory of you? Why?

28.   If all jobs paid the same wages, what job would you most like to have? Why?

29. Looking into the future, will cooperation and violence between people remain the same, or will it change? Why, or why not?

30. If you had to make a choice, would you want your future career to make you wealthy, very helpful to others, or give you 100% daily satisfaction? Why?

31. Is an incredibly strong desire all you need to achieve what you want? Why, or why not?

32. Is there really such a thing as reincarnation? How can you tell?

33. Your name is in the 1st page headline of tomorrow's newspaper. What does the headline say?

34. What work would you love to be involved in full-time as an adult, even if you did not get paid for it? Why?

35. Would you like to be known as the "World's Oldest Living Person"? Why, or why not?

36. You are a promoter and agent of a presently-unknown person, and make them into a famous star. What do they become famous for doing or being?

37. What modern-day device do you think may not be around when your grandchildren are your age? Why?

38. What are your two greatest concerns about the future? How can you take charge of those concerns?

39. If you knew the exact time you were going to die, what three things would you want to first do or accomplish? Why?

40. How much money will your autograph be worth 50 years from now? Why?

41. What is the oldest item in your house right now? Will you help preserve it when you are older? Why, or why not?

42. If you could become famous for either acting, music or sports, which would you choose? Why?

43. Many people today complain that life isn't "fair." In future generations, do you think life will be fair for people? Why, or why not?

44. At a Chinese restaurant, you receive a fortune cookie. You see that it has to do with your future. What does it say?

45. Years from now your children may be in many school events. As their parent, what involvement or participation will you have in their activities? Why, or why not?

46. Some people use a ball as the main tool in their profession; others use a pen; still others use a microphone. What will be the main item you use in your future career? Why?

47. Do you think your present ideas of how to "party" will change as you get older? If so, in what ways?

48. How much influence should parents have in what their child does after high school graduation? Why, or why not?

49. If you could choose one person to remain in contact with the entire rest of your life, who would you choose? Why?

50. What is one New Year's resolution that you have kept? How difficult was it?

51. To get where you want to be 10 years from now, is college important in helping you to reach your goals? Why, or why not?

52. Forty years from now, how will you know whether you will have had a successful life?

53. When you are an adult, will wealth, fame, happiness, or something else be the sign that you were successful? Why is that important to you?

54. In future generations, do you think recycling of unwanted items will be a thing of the past, or will people find a way to re-use all refuse? What gives you that idea?

55. Peering into the future, do you see in your child's or grandchild's lifetime, advanced computer technology replacing all paper and writing instruments? Why, or why not?

56. A highly advanced mirror is developed, by which anyone standing in front of it can automatically view how they would look 50 years from that moment. If you had the opportunity, would you use this mirror? Why, or why not?

57. In your grandchild's lifetime, do you think our oceans or neighboring planets will be colonized first? What gives you that idea?

58. From what you have experienced so far, do you think discrimination will improve or worsen from your generation to your child's? How can you tell? What part can you play?

59. When you are an adult, do you think your career will be as important to you as your family, or will one be more important than the other? If so, which one, and why?

60. What is the one thing you would most like to learn before you die? Why?

61. If you lived 100 years ago, what job do you think you would have had? Why?

62. If you had the opportunity to peer into the future to find the answer, what question would you most want answered? Why is it so important?

Perfection

1. What is a talent another person has that you envy? Why?

2. Would you rather own a boat, a car, or a plane? Why?

3. If you could trade places with anyone for 24 hours, who would it be? Why?

4. If you could invite a famous person home for supper, who would you choose? ...what would you serve? Why?

5. If you could change one thing in your family, what would it be? Why?

6. What is the IDEAL age? Why?

7. If a radio station played your favorite song request non-stop, what would the song be? Why?

8. For any sports, social, or academic subject, what would you want to win "The World's Greatest _____" medal in? Why?

9. What could be another type of network to add to satellite or cable TV? Why?

10. What is the best topping to put on a baked potato?

11. If you won 2 free tickets, for what would you like them to be? Why?

12. If you had a job in a department store, what department would you want to work in? Why?

13. In the future, you can take a pill to give you total knowledge in one subject. Which pill would you take? Why?

14. ...what would you do with all that knowledge?

15. What is a gift you would like to find waiting at home for you tomorrow? Why?

16. What message would you like to have flying on a banner over your house? Why?

17. What movie is worth watching 20 times? Why?

18. What is the best thing to cook or roast over a campfire? Why?

19. What possession would you not sell for any price? Why not?

20. If there were a 25th hour added to each day, how would you spend it? Why?

21. Describe "perfect."

22. Do you know anything that is "perfect"?

23. Describe your idea of a "perfect" day.

24. Which is the best seat in a movie theater? How can you tell?

25. If you had the chance to be on a TV talk show, what topic would you want to talk about most? Why?

26. Would you rather be taller or shorter than you are right now? Why?

27. Do you have an "ideal" height and/or weight in mind for yourself? If so, what gives you that idea?

28. If you could live anywhere in the world for the rest of your life, where would it be? Why?

29. If you were to adopt a different name, what would it be? Why?

30. If the story of your life were to be made into a novel, what would the title be? Why?

31. What would have to happen for you to be completely happy? Why?

32. Where would you say is the most relaxing spot on earth? Why?

33. If you could spend a year studying one animal, which creature would you choose? Why?

34. What is your idea of a comfortable life?

35. You win a 15-minute free food-grab at a grocery store. How would you spend your 15 minutes? Why?

36. If you had just one more hour to live, ideally, how would you most like to spend it? Why?

37. If you were to start your own band or group, what style of music would be your group's specialty? Why?

38. What is the most important thing you have ever told someone?

39. If you could choose your family's next vacation spot, where would you pick? Why?

40. What is the most necessary item to have at a party? Why?

41. If you could take a pill doubling the ability of one of your 5 senses, which sense would you want to increase? Why?

42. If you had the opportunity, whose private diary would you like to read? Why?

43. You are employed at Walt Disney World to create a brand new, popular attraction. What would you create? Why?

44. Is bigger always better? Why, or why not?

45. Is it possible to be too nice? If so, is that a bad thing?

46. How would you plan the ultimate party? Why?

47. You have the chance to "pig out" on your favorite snack. What snack would you fix? Why?

48. If you could change your most obvious physical flaw, would you? Is it as noticeable to others as it is to you?

49. Your assignment is to create a new comic book character and make it unlike any other in present comics. How would your character be different? Why?

50. If your picture was to be printed on the cover of a national magazine, which magazine would you want it to be? For what reason?

51. If you were offered one major adventure, would you choose to go on a trip into outer space or deep into the ocean? Why?

52. If you could regularly produce either a newspaper, magazine, or CD's, which would you choose? Why?

53. If you could be granted a life-time supply of any one item, what would you choose? Why?

54. Architecture Today wants you to write an article describing the perfect bedroom for someone your age. What would your article say? Why?

55. Who, to you, seems to have the perfect life? Why?

56. What day was so special that you want to remember it for the rest of your life? Why?

57. Who would you give the "World's Most Patient Person" award to? Why?

58. If you could start your own business, what kind would it be? Why?

59. If you could have one dance with anyone in the world, who would you choose? Why?

60. Your school principal is scheduling someone to give an inspiring talk to your whole school. If it was your decision, who would you invite? Why?

61. If you had the opportunity (and extra cash), what would you like to extravagantly buy, even if only once? Why?

62. You have an opportunity to plan and direct the next music video of your favorite singer or group. Who would you want most to work with? Why?

63. Which music video, in your opinion, is the greatest of all time? What makes it so outstanding?

64. Your local shopping mall is hiring. If you were applying for a job, which store at the mall would you most want to work in? Why?

65. How would you describe the perfect pizza?

66. Our nation's lawmakers may make plans to change the portrait on the $1 bill, and ask for suggestions. Whose portrait would you suggest be the new face on the bill? Why?

67. After this activity, you are scheduled to board a private jet and fly anywhere you want. Where would you choose to go? Why?

68. You find yourself stuck in an elevator with one other person. To make time pass as easily as possible, what type of person would you want them to be? Why?

69. Which exotic animal would you like to have for a pet, if it were allowed? Why?

70. Ideally, under your yearbook senior picture, how would you finish the caption, "The person most likely..." Why?

71. What type of TV show would you be perfect to emcee? Why?

72. For your birthday, you are promised your favorite breakfast. What would that breakfast be? Who would you want to be there? Why?

73. What is a gift you would like to find waiting for you when you get home today? Why?

74. What is your favorite way to spend New Year's Eve? Why?

75. What would be the ingredients in the most delicious ice cream sundae you could create?

76. Your younger cousin asks you to describe what "normal" means. How would you respond?

77. What is the most ideal way to spend a Saturday night? Why?

78. You plan to spend an entire night at home with your friends doing a one-celebrity video/movie marathon. Assuming it's your choice, who would you spend the evening watching? Why?

79. Who, presently, is your role model? In what way, or ways?

80. What are the characteristics of your "ideal" teacher? Has anyone come close?

81. What are the characteristics of the "ideal" student? How close do you come?

82. What are the characteristics of the ideal coach?

83. You and a friend plan to start a radio station that will be very unique. To get a good listening audience, how would your station be different from others? Why?

84. What would be your ideal after-school job? In what ways would it be the best?

85. What is the best CD album for any party? Why?

86. What would be your ideal way to spend a weekend? Why?

87. If you had the opportunity to rise one hour earlier than anyone else in your family, how would you spend that time? Why?

88. Which brand of tennis shoe is the best? Why?

89. In the future, there may be many more Halls of Fame for a variety of reasons. Ideally, into which Hall of Fame would you wish to be voted? Why?

90. What is your favorite kind of sandwich to make? Why?

91.   If, at a restaurant, you could order the most elegant, first-class meal possible, what would you order? Why?

92.   What is the greatest thing you have ever won? What made it so special?

93.   You are going to write a book that will make the national Best Seller list. Who or what will your book be about? Why?

94.   If you were given $500 with no strings attached, what would you do with it? Why?

95.   If you could put only one more thing in your refrigerator, what would it be? Why?

—— if anybody asks me...

Social Topics

1. Why would you walk out of a movie?

2. How would you feel if the law said everyone HAD to have guns in their house? Why?

3. Who is someone you would pay $100 to meet? Why?

4. What is something people seem to take for granted? Why does it seem so?

5. Whose autograph would you spend $100 to get? Why?

6. Who is a hero of yours today? Why?

7. How good a thing is gambling? Why, or why not?

8. What kind of gambling is acceptable? When is gambling not okay?

9. What makes a person a hero? Why?

10. Why do most of today's heroes seem to be sports people rather than doctors or scientists?

11. After complaining about the way everyone is mistreating them, your younger cousin wants you to explain what "fair" means. What do you tell them?

12. What does "respect" mean to you? Why?

13. How much TV is too much?

14. Should TV be rated for young people? Why, or why not?

15. Should CDs be rated for young people? Why, or why not?

16. Should kids be allowed to vote in national elections? Why, or why not?

17. If you made a super-huge donation to a charity, would you want it to stay anonymous, or be made known to the public? Why?

18. What is one magazine everyone should subscribe to? Why?

19. What one book should everyone read? Why?

20. What is one law you would like to see changed? Why?

21. What is one idea that should be made law? Why?

22. Should movie stars be paid the millions they get for acting? Why, or why not?

23. What is the most dangerous kind of drug? In what way?

24. What is the difference between right and wrong?

25. Should the Internet be censored for younger viewers? Why, or why not?

26. Who should monitor young people's use of the Internet? Why?

27. How much money makes you rich? Why that amount?

28. Who is the best dancer you know? What kind of dance do they do?

29. What would be the most interesting foreign language to learn? Why?

30. What new color of M&M® should be added to the bag? Why?

31. Should everyone be rich? If not, who should be?

32. How much education should a person get? Why?

33. Should everyone strive to get as much formal education as they can? Why, or why not?

34. Which movies are better: "G" rated or "R" rated? Why?

35. What is the difference between someone who is brave and someone who is foolish? Why?

36. If you were given $1000 that had to be spent, and not kept in any form for you, how would you use it? Why?

37. What person do you think should be printed on the next U.S. postage stamp? Why?

38. Should laboratory experiments with animals continue in order to develop vaccines for humans? Why, or why not?

39. You can interview one person to learn and report about their life story? Who would you choose? Why?

40. At what age should someone be allowed to get a part-time job? Why?

41. Should young children be taken to a funeral service? Why, or why not?

42. Could four or five families, all of different cultural backgrounds, live in the same neighborhood? ...what kind of difficulties might arise?

43. What kind of animal should not be hunted? Why?

44. Are athletes worth the large amounts of money they are paid? Why, or why not?

45. Is there any crime for which a criminal should be given the death penalty? Why, or why not?

46. Should a criminal go to prison as punishment, or be reeducated with more appropriate behaviors and attitudes? Why?

47. Should foreign immigrants continue to be allowed to enter the U.S. as freely as they do now? Why, or why not?

48. As an adult, would you choose to live next to a family just moving in from a foreign country? Why, or why not?

49. Should department stores control the style of music they will and won't sell to the public? Why, or why not?

50. In your opinion, which kind of music should be banned? Why?

51. What kinds of things should not be shown on TV? Why?

52. Do adults get enough respect from today's youth? Why, or why not?

53. Should all TV be family-oriented and G-rated? Why, or why not?

54. What new national holiday could be added to our calendar? Why?

55. What picture comes to mind when you hear the word "torture"? Why?

56. What does it mean to be an alcoholic? Why?

57. What is something about another person that seems acceptable to make fun of? Why?

58.   A business manager has a choice of hiring two part-time teenagers cheaply, or an adult who has a family and house. What do you think the manager should decide? Why?

59.   Which medium—radio, TV, or newspaper— influences U.S. people the most? How can you tell?

60.   If you were to organize a letter-writing project to encourage people to try to change a bad situation, what major problem would you tackle? Why?

61.   Is it alright to have graffiti written in or on public places? Why, or why not?

62.   From what you have seen, who takes better care of the environment—children or adults? How can you tell?

63.   Many cities operate a Teen Court, made up of responsible teenagers who sit in judgment of other teens that have broken the law, and also to establish the punishment or fine for the youthful offender. Would you like to see a Teen Court operating in your town? Why, or why not?

64. Should a store take back anything a customer returns, for the customer's satisfaction? Why, or why not?

65. How old should someone be before they can legally gamble? Why?

66. Should activities that are definitely harmful for kids (i.e., smoking, drinking, gambling, etc.) still be allowed for adults? Why, or why not?

67. If it was your decision, how much money would you have the U.S. spend each year for space exploration? Why?

68. From your experience, is life reflected in movies, or are movies reflected in real life? How can you tell?

69. What two characteristics of a movie help you decide that it is definitely worth going to see? Why?

70. Should driving privileges automatically be removed from adults when they reach a certain age? Why, or why not?

71. Can some T-shirt messages really be offensive? Why?

72. What is one senseless commercial you have come across that you wish the advertisers would improve? Why?

73. What is a topic or problem that you think is worth physically fighting for? Why?

74. Is it alright for adults to swear, and then teach their children not to? Why, or why not?

75. From your experience, does money solve problems or create them? How can you tell?

76. We often think we are right when a crowd agrees with us. Is there a time, though, when the crowd could be wrong? If so, when?

77. Can famous people be photographed too much? How much is too much?

78. Should there be more or less "no smoking" spaces in public restaurants? Why?

79. Tobacco companies can no longer advertise on TV because of the number of youthful viewers. Should a similar law apply to alcoholic beverages? Why, or why not?

80. What is the difference between a "group" and a "gang" of people?

81. At a restaurant, you hear everyone at a nearby booth laughing and conversing in an unfamiliar language. What would your thoughts be? Why?

82. Are $150 tennis shoes better than $50 tennis shoes? Why, or why not?

83. Should the legal age for drinking be raised, lowered, or stay the same? Why?

84. Should the legal age for voting be raised, lowered, or stay the same? Why?

85. There is concern about the young age at which children are entered in beauty pageants. Should there be an age restriction placed on participants? Why, or why not?

86. How much time on the Internet is too much? Why?

87. Should there be a law prohibiting anyone from burning the American flag? Why, or why not?

88. It seems like most of your friends are, or want to be, on a diet. They all have their reasons. What, in your mind, is a reason for a person to NOT go on a diet? Why?

89. In a few years you will be a famous individual. How can you balance your private life with your fans' interest to be with you and know all about you?

90. Could music videos improve to be even more entertaining and remain tasteful? If so, how?

91. Should music videos be rated as movies are, or are they appropriate for all ages? Why?

92. To you, which is the most important network on cable or satellite TV? Why?

93. Two of your friends are applying for the same job. One of them has had the identical job before and, therefore, valuable experience. The other has never worked, but their dad owns the company. If you had to make the decision, who would you hire? Why?

94. What do you think about people who color their hair? Why?

95. Should all buildings be off-limits to smokers? Why, or why not? If not, what would be a reasonable solution? Why?

96. A teen in your neighborhood has been arrested for committing a serious crime. Many people are blaming his mistake on bad family upbringing. Should his legal punishment take into account any family history, such as poor parenting? Why, or why not?

97. Should movie theaters allow some food and drink to be brought in? Why, or why not?

98. Should there be a "Take Your Son to Work Day," just as there is for daughters? Why, or why not?

99. You hear that, in view of increasing violence at schools, your school will be installing metal detectors to uncover weapons brought on the grounds. Do you think this is a good idea? Why, or why not?

100. What is a fair and adequate policy for using air bags in cars? Why?

101. How do you think the laws or policies in our country would change if the voting age was lowered to 12? Would this be an improvement? Why, or why not?

102.   Does a person have the right to total self-expression, in any way, under any circumstances? If not, where would you draw the line? Why?

103.   Should female recruits in the army go through the very same training in preparation for combat as the male recruits? Why, or why not?

104.   Should there be tighter gun control in our country? Why, or why not?

105.   Could a woman be just as efficient a U.S. president as a man? Why, or why not?

106.   When do you think the U.S. will have its first female president? How do you think this will change things?

107.   Should prayer, or some form of it, be allowed in public schools? Why, or why not?

108.   When you are about to become a parent, your spouse and you will have the opportunity to learn the sex of the child and whether it has any abnormalities. How much of this information would you want to know? Why, or why not?

109. Is it helpful to know, before birth, whether an unborn fetus will have any physical or mental abnormalities? Why, or why not?

110. Your friend takes a table knife out of a bag at lunch to cut up food. Immediately, the knife is taken away, and your friend is sent to the Principal's office. The result is suspension for bringing a weapon to school and violating school policy. Does this seem a reasonable and effective policy? Why, or why not? If not, how could it be revised to be more appropriate and still effective in maintaining safety at school?

111. Should parents be allowed to officially train and certify their own children for a driver's license? Why, or why not?

112. Some people say that getting angry is a waste of time and energy. Would you agree? Why, or why not?

113. What is the main reason you think so many teenagers take up smoking?

114. What is an acceptable reason for smoking?

115.   To control the violence children see on TV, many people want a V-chip to be automatically added to the TV. Others feel it is the parents' duty to control the shows children watch. Which idea makes more sense to you? Why?

116.   Which area of daily news would you say you follow the least: local, state, national, or world? Why?

117.   Children you are baby-sitting surprise you by making several derogatory comments about a particular race or culture; you learn that these are comments they have heard from their parents. What would you do or say? Why, or why not?

—— if anybody asks me...

1.   ...how neat a person are you?

2.   ...how well can you keep a secret?

3.   ...how likely are you to take chances?

4.   ...how easy is it for you to accept criticism?

5.   ...how much do you believe in astrology?

6.   ...how forgiving are you?

7.   ...how punctual are you?

8.   ...how important is respect?

9.   ...how difficult is it for you to apologize?

10.   ...how organized are you?

11.   ...how well do you obey your parents?

12.   ...how trustworthy are you?

13.   ...how important is it to be popular?

14.   ...how much do you like to make your own decisions?

15.   ...how much do you trust your parents?

16. ...how much do you think your parents trust you?

17. ...how easy is it for you to make new friends?

18. ...how important is it to keep a clean bedroom?

19. ...how well do you like to see your image in the mirror?

20. ...how easy is it for you to stand up for your personal beliefs?

21. ...how helpful is spanking in a family?

22. ...how would you rate your life right now?

23. ...how much do you judge others by their appearance?

24. ...how much privacy do you get at home?

25. ...how safe do you feel at your school?

26. ...how comfortable are you in "showing off" your parents to your friends?

27. ...how much do you need to be "in charge" of things?

28.   ...how good/effective is communication between most teenagers and adults today?

29.   ...how easy is it for you to accept defeat?

30.   ...how important is it to learn a second or third language?

31.   ...how "physical" do you become when you are angry?

32.   ...how important do you feel it is for you to know what is happening in the world?

33.   ...how important is perfect school attendance to you?

34.   ...how easy is it for you to give up something to a person in need?

35.   ...how concerned are you about what you wear in public?

36.   ...how comfortable are you with nicknames people give you?

37.   ...how much of an exercise fanatic are you?

38.   ...how easily do you get headaches?

39. ...how proud are you of the way you deal with your enemies?

40. ...how big of a problem do you think child abuse is today?

41. ...how important is it for you to wear an expensive pair of gym shoes?

42. ...how difficult would it be for you to return the extra change handed to you?

43. ...how boring is your life right now?

44. ...how important is it to you to attend a four-year college?

45. ...how important is it for parents to attend the activities and events of their kids?

46. ...how much personal control do you have over your reputation with friends?

47. ...how comfortable is it for you to openly disagree with your friends?

48. ...how much can your peers depend on you?

49. ...how much school pride do you have?

50. ...how easy is it for you to recover when you make a mistake in a game?

51. ...how good/effective are your study skills?

52. ...how important is religion to you right now?

53. ...how "open" a person are you?

54. ...how impulsive are you?

55. ...how easily do you get embarrassed?

56. ...how much of a "party person" are you?

57. ...how easy is it for you to save money?

58. ...how comfortable are you with having your picture taken?

59. ...how firm are your parents once they have made a decision?

60. ...how easy is it for you to talk your parents into things?

61. ...how likely are you to lend out your homework to others?

62. ...how much should people be judged by their past?

63. ...how likely are you to give up your seat to someone you don't know while on a crowded bus?

64. ...how likely are you to return a bad meal at a restaurant to the kitchen?

65. ...how much are you consulted in family decisions?

66. ...how easy is it to obey your parents?

67. ...how bad might you feel to find out some people don't like you?

68. ...how much of the "real you" do your friends know?

69. ...how easy do you think it is for parents to let their newly-licensed teen drive the family car?

70. ...how much do you worry about what will, or might, happen?

71. ...how important is a good, deep summer tan to you?

72. ...how likely are you, at home, to eat a very nutritious meal you just don't like?

73.   ...how important will family reunions be when you are an adult?

74.   ...how easy is it to show respect to someone not respecting you?

75.   ...how dependable are you?

76.   ...how well do your parents understand your daily concerns and troubles?

77.   ...how important is it to you to have a good relationship with your friends' parents?

78.   ...how much are students at your school judged by their clothes?

—— if anybody asks me...

What if... —

1. ...there were no rules?

2. ...school were year-round?

3. ...there was no paper?

4. ...there was only one TV channel?

5. ...everyone had a 6th sense. What might it be?

6. ...each job paid the same amount of money?

7. ...there were no mirrors?

8. ...students could get a high school diploma only if they earn a "C" or better in all classes?

9. ...students could move up to the next grade only if they earned a "C" or better in all classes?

10. ...you did not get a grade for your classes; only Pass-Fail evaluations?

11. ...your parents had a job requiring the family to move each year?

12. ...your school required students to wear uniforms?

13. ...each athlete in high school sports got equal playing time?

14. ...the legal age for a driver's license was lowered to 14?

15. ...teachers were given year-end evaluations by their students?

16. ...no homework was ever given?

17. ...your friends all thought of your house as "home base"?

18. ...your school had no required courses; rather, all classes were electives?

19. ...you had 100% total, perfect memory of everything you have experienced in life?

20. ...your school did not create any honor role list or class ranking?

21. ...working teenagers paid for a portion of the family food bill?

22. ...shopping malls required a "cover charge" at the entrance?

23. ...public education stopped at age 14?

24.   ...you woke up tomorrow morning and found no one else in the house?

25.   ...each family member regularly handed to each other a "How Am I Doing?" card, similar to those used in restaurants and hotels?

26.   ...there were no public water fountains, as is the case in many foreign countries?

27.   ...all children were home-schooled daily by computer technology?

28.   ...scores were never kept during games?

—— if anybody asks me...

other ideas ———

—— if anybody asks me...

—— if anybody asks me...

—— if anybody asks me...